Su

of

Just Mercy
Bryan Stevenson

Conversation Starters

By BookHabits

Please Note: This is an unofficial conversation starters guide. If you have not yet read the original work or would like to read it again, get the book here.

We hope you enjoy this complementary guide from BookHabits.
Our mission is to aid readers and reading groups with quality, thought provoking material to in the discovery and discussions on some of today's favorite books.

Tips for Using BookHabits Conversation Starters:

EVERY GOOD BOOK CONTAINS A WORLD FAR DEEPER THAN the surface of its pages. The characters and their world come alive through the words on the pages, yet the characters and its world still live on. Questions herein are designed to bring us beneath the surface of the page and invite us into the world that lives on. These questions can be used to:

- Foster a deeper understanding of the book
- Promote an atmosphere of discussion for groups
- Assist in the study of the book, either individually or corporately
- Explore unseen realms of the book as never seen before

About Us:

THROUGH YEARS OF EXPERIENCE AND FIELD EXPERTISE, from newspaper featured book clubs to local library chapters, *BookHabits* can bring your book discussion to life. Host your book party as we discuss some of today's most widely read books.

Table of Contents

Introducing *Just Mercy*

*J*UST *MERCY* IS BRYAN STEVENSON'S JOURNEY THROUGH the morass and injustices of the American justice system. A lawyer who quickly became interested in civil rights, Stevenson decided to join the SPDC, an organization whose mission was to assist the prisoners on death row in the American South. Gradually, Stevenson finds himself sucked into the problems of his clients and begins to work full time on cases in which he considers the punishments were harsh and disproportionate with the crime.

The book follows the story of Walter McMillian, an innocent man who was framed for the murder of a white girl because he had dared to have an affair with another white woman. Walter spent six years on death row for a crime he didn't commit and was finally released through the efforts of Stevenson and his team. During this time, Stevenson uncovered not just incompetency in the law enforcement and legal system, but blatant corruption, racism, and unwillingness to find the truth. Walter received a minuscule amount of compensation for his troubles and ended his days with dementia, diagnosed to have been brought on by the trauma he had undergone during his incarceration.

Though Walter's story takes primacy in the book, it is interspersed with the stories of other victims of the justice system. Through these cases, Stevenson shows how the system was based on racism, sexism, and poverty. One of the things Stevenson has been fighting against is the execution of minors, something that only a handful of countries in the world practice, the US being one of them. The country has hundreds of children on death row, and others have spent decades in prison with no hope of parole or release for minor crimes. Some of the children were innocent of the crimes of which they had been accused.

Stevenson also talks about women who gave birth to stillborn children and found themselves in prison for decades. There have been witch hunts for "bad" mothers who have tried to hide their pregnancies for fear of social censure and have then given birth to stillbirth children. Many of these women also had no access to abortions, prenatal care, and general health care. Pregnancy-related mental illnesses such as postpartum depression were not discussed or acknowledged in the cases of women who had harmed their children. All this increased the chances of women being targeted unfairly in order to fill the prisons.

Stevenson also discusses how there is little to no help for people suffering from mental illnesses and drug abuse. People who need help are thrown into prison for years instead of receiving the help that would help them become productive members of the society again.

The prison industry that has risen up has made incarceration a business and this business model requires that more and more people be put behind bars for silly to non-existent reasons. The focus of this kind of economy-driven justice system means that justice is not served either for the victim or the perpetrator. Instead, a whole new generation of criminals is being created by poverty, racism, gender inequality, and other social injustices.

Discussion Questions

"Get Ready to Enter a New World"

Tip: Begin with questions dealing with broader issues to ensure ample time for quality discussions. Read through all discussion questions before engaging.

~~~

question 1

What do you think the title of the book, *Just Mercy*, refers to? Stevenson believes that mercy must be given to the undeserving. What do you think of this concept? Do you believe in mercy for those who have committed crimes? Why or why not?

~~~

~ ~ ~

question 2

The book talks about the different ways in which being poor increases your chance of going to prison. How do you think the government and society can deal with this problem? Why do you think poor people get into petty crime? Discuss.

~ ~ ~

question 3

Walter McMillian was deliberately framed for murder by the law enforcement authorities and the prosecutor without any apparent reason. Why do you think this happened? Is being a black man sufficient to get an obviously innocent man into prison? What other factors do you think are at play here?

~~~

question 4

The US has a unique history with respect to slavery and racism. How do you think this history has shaped the way society functions in the US today? How do you think the country and the people can rise above their history?

~~~

~~~

question 5

One of the reasons cited by Stevenson for the large incarceration numbers in the US is the prison industry and its lobby. What kind of reforms do you think the country requires to make the justice system really about justice, and not about profit? What other problems do you think needs to be solved to make these reforms more effective?

~~~

~~~

question 6

The US has one of the highest incarceration rates in the world. Do you think putting more people in prisons is beneficial to the society at large? What kind of people do you think need to be in prison, according to you? Discuss.

~~~

question 7

Stevenson discusses many cases in which juvenile offenders are tried as adults. What do you think is the logic behind this treatment? Do you think this helps the entire society as a whole? How can juvenile crime be prevented in the first place?

question 8

The US justice system is focused on punishment instead of rehabilitation and reintegration. What kind of criminals do you think cannot be rehabilitated at all? Name any case in which you think that the offender could not have been rehabilitated and state your reasons why.

~~~

question 9

The author vehemently speaks out against the death penalty. What are the alternatives to this in cases where the offender has few chances of being rehabilitated? Is keeping a human being in a prison cage any more humane than executing them? What is the most humane alternative in these cases, according to you? Discuss.

~~~

question 10

Many of the children who end up in adult prisons come from a background of poverty, abuse, and neglect. In one case, a boy called Charlie killed his mother's abuser and was tried as an adult and kept in an adult prison, where he was raped. How can one ensure the safety of incarcerated children in these cases? What do you think is the logic behind trying children as adults?

~ ~ ~

~~~

question 11

The US, along with Iran, Yemen, Nigeria, Pakistan, Saudi Arabia, China, and Congo make up the handful of countries in the world that allow the death penalty for children. What do you think are the similarities among these countries that allow children to be executed without giving them a chance to rehabilitate?

~~~

question 12

Stevenson discusses the case of Herbert Richardson, a war veteran, who was stalking a woman and then killed two little girls after a misguided plan to save the woman from a bomb and earning her love went wrong. How do you think can the streets be made safer for women from predators like Herbert? How can a balance be found between the safety of women and the human rights of mentally ill predators?

~~~

question 13

In the US, immunity is given to law enforcement, judges, and prosecutors from prosecution in cases of wrongful imprisonment even if they indulged in illegal practices or blatantly framed innocent people even after knowing the facts. How far should immunity to these professionals be granted from mistakes, according to you?

~~~

question 14

There are a lot of women who spend decades in prison because they give birth to stillbirth children. Why do you think there is a paranoia regarding such women, and what kind of initiatives can be taken to reduce this kind of arbitrary sentencing targeting women?

~~~

question 15

What kind of social reforms and ideological changes to the society do you think are necessary for the US to bring about a kinder and more humane justice system that focuses on rehabilitation and prevention rather than punishment and incarceration? Discuss.

~~~

question 16

The *New York Times* featured a review by Ted Conover in which he compares Bryan Stevenson to Paul Farmer. What do you know about Paul Farmer? In what ways are the achievements of these two men similar?

question 17

The review in *The New York Times* by Ted Conover claims that one of the faults of the book is that it recounts stories that took place over 30 years ago as if they happened yesterday. What do you think about this? Do you agree this is the perception given by *Just Mercy*? Why, or why not?

~~~

question 18

Bryan Stevenson has been accused of not acknowledging his clients' dark side by reviewer Ted Conover in *The New York Times*. He cites the cases of teenage arson, which results in two deaths, and a stalker who kills two young girls when he placed a bomb on his victim's porch. In both these cases, Stevenson makes excuses for the perpetrators according to Conover. Do you agree this is the case? What is the best way to deal with such cases?

~ ~ ~

~~~

question 19

Rob Warden from *The Washington Post* claims that Alabama is the worst state in the US for incompetent, uninformed, and prejudiced judgments. Why do you think he says this? Which state do you think has worse problems than Alabama, if any, and why?

~~~

~~~

question 20

The Washington Post published a review of *Just Mercy*, in which reviewer Rob Warden claims that the show *60 Minutes* was a major ally in Walter's fight for justice. How far do you think the show helped his case? Discuss.

~~~

Introducing the Author

BRYAN STEVENSON IS AN AMERICAN LAWYER WHO FIGHTS against racism, sexism, ineptitude, and deliberate systemic abuse of incarcerated people in the justice system. Born black in Delaware during the Jim Crow era, Stevenson firsthand saw how the concepts of crime and punishment were applied differently to people from different social strata.

He went to a colored only school, which was desegregated when he entered second grade. However, the segregation still applied as the white students would not interact with the black students and the latter were forced to use different facilities. Stevenson was a good student and was offered a scholarship to attend Eastern University, where he studied psychology. Later, he went on to Harvard Law School, where he was offered afull scholarship.

It was during his time at Harvard that Stevenson became interested in law as a driving force for social justice when he attended a class on poverty and race litigation. He also decided to do an internship at the Southern Center for Human Rights, a government funded organization representing people incarcerated on death row in the American South. He got involved in this initiative and was soon running the center. Funding was cut off in 1994, so he founded the Equal Justice Initiative, which did the same work but received funding from different sources.

Apart from dealing with death-row inmates, the main focus of Stevenson's work was to work with people incarcerated with overly harsh sentences for juvenile crimes. He has achieved a lot of success in getting major laws changed in this area, and is trying to put a stop to the sentencing of children as adults by courts around the country.

Stevenson is also very active in preserving slave history and showcasing its impact on the population, which has led the US to its current situation. He is also working to build a memorial in

Montgomery to commemorate the lynchings of black people over the decades in the South.

For his relentless activism, Stevenson has been granted a MacArthur Fellowship, Olof Palme Prize, Gruber Justice Prize, and Four Freedoms Award. He also received an honorary doctorate from Williams College and an honorary Doctor of Law degree from the University of Delaware for his social justice work.

Fireside Questions

"What would you do?"

Tip: These questions can be a fun exercise as it spurs creativity among the readers by allowing alternate scene endings and "if this was you" questions.

~~~

question 21

In *The New York Review of Books*, the reviewer David Cole compares *Just Mercy* to the fiction book, *To Kill a Mockingbird*. What parallels can you draw between these two books? What are the differences?

~~~

~~~

question 22

Reviewer David Cole from *The New York Review of Books* echoes Stevenson's point that no one is as bad as the worst thing he has ever done. Do you agree with this? How can this concept be applied to the criminal justice system?

~~~

~~~

question 23

In his review, David Cole from *The New York Review of Books* attributes the mass incarceration culture in the US to the absence of empathy. Do you agree? What other factors do you think contribute to this phenomenon?

~~~

question 24

Book Page featured a review in which the reviewer calls *Just Mercy* a call to arms. What do you think is the context behind this opinion? Discuss.

question 25

Reviewer Don Herzog from *The New Rambler* points out that the problem with Stevenson's view on the death penalty is that we generally think of mercy and justice as conflicting ideas. Can you explain the context behind these words?

question 26

Stevenson calls himself broken, which is why he feels the need to continue working for other people's human rights. In what way do you think he feels broken?

~~~

question 27

Stevenson was born during the Jim Crow era and experienced segregation and racism to the ultimate. After desegregation, he was able to complete his education and attain scholarships to go to university. How do you think he would have fared if desegregation had not happened?

~~~

question 28

Stevenson believes that the death penalty must not be used in a civilized country. Do you agree with him? Why or why not?

~~~

question 29

Stevenson claims that slavery, the terror reign after reconstruction, segregation, and mass incarceration are the four institutions in the US that have shaped their ideas of justice. Which one do you think is the most potent in maintaining status quo in the US and why?

~~~

question 30

Funding for the Southern Center for Human Rights was cut off in 1994. What do you think was the reason for this?

~~~

question 31

Stevenson's grandfather was murdered by two teenagers. Yet he grew up to become a defender of the rights of children in prison for similar crimes. Under similar circumstances, how do you think you would react, and why?

~~~

question 32

Stevenson talks about a time when he was taken to be a convict by the judge and the prosecutor just because he was white. Stevenson manages to pass it off with a smile. How do you think you would have reacted in the situation? What would have been the consequences for Stevenson if he had protested?

~~~

question 33

Take any case that has been in the papers and imagine you were involved in the case as the convicted. Then imagine your race is different than what it is and discuss how it would change your prospects in court.

~~~

question 34

Walter MacMillan was convicted and received a vicious sentence because he was black and had an affair with a white woman. If he had been of a different race other than black or white, do you think he would have been persecuted in the same manner? Why or why not?

~~~

~~~

question 35

Stevenson wanted to work with prisoners on death row and also focused on working with children who were given harsh sentences for juvenile crimes. If you had to invest your time in a social cause close to your heart, which one would it be, and why?

~~~

question 36

Pick any country of your choice other than the US. Take the case of Herbert Stevenson who was stalking a woman and killed two young girls when he planted a bomb at her front porch. What would be the result of the trial in this country, according to you, and why?

~~~

question 37

Stevenson observes that many of the black convicts on death row had been convicted on flimsy grounds by an all-white jury. If the jury had been more diverse, what aspects would be taken by them in considering the case, according to you?

~~~

question 38

Black Americans make up a disproportionate percentage of the incarcerated in the country. If slavery had not existed and they had voluntarily entered the US for employment, how do you think their development as a community would have taken place?

~~~

Quiz Questions

"Ready to Announce the Winners?"

Tip: Create a leaderboard and track scores to see who gets the most correct answers. Winners required. Prizes optional.

quiz question 1

True or False: Marsha Colbey's case shows the need for stringent action against mothers.

~~~

quiz question 2

Trina Garnett was convicted for _____.

~~~

~~~

quiz question 3

Evan Miller's victim gave him _____.

~~~

quiz question 4

True or False: Walter MacMillan was guilty of murder.

quiz question 5

Antonio Nuñez wanted to be a _____ when he grew up.

quiz question 6

Joe Sullivan was convicted for _____.

~~~

~~~

quiz question 7

True or False: Walter MacMillan spent six years in prison.

~~~

quiz question 8

True or False: Stevenson worked with children who were convicted as adults.

~ ~ ~

~~~

quiz question 9

Stevenson started the nonprofit organization
_____.

~~~

quiz question 10

Stevenson did most of his work in _____.

~~~

quiz question 11

True or False: Stevenson was born in Alabama.

~~~

~~~

quiz question 12

Stevenson studied law at _____.

~~~

Quiz Answers

1. False; the case shows the systemic sexism against women, holding them responsible for having stillbirths.
2. Arson
3. Drugs
4. False; Walter MacMillan was framed for the murder, and the real murderer was never caught.
5. Police officer
6. Rape and sexual battery
7. True
8. False; Walter MacMillan was framed for the murder, and the real murderer was never caught.
9. Equal Justice Initiative
10. Alabama
11. False; he was born in Delaware.
12. Harvard Law School

Ways to Continue Your Reading

EVERY month, our team runs through a wide selection of books to pick the best titles for readers and reading groups, and promotes these titles to our thousands of readers – sometimes with free downloads, sale dates, and additional brochures.

If you have not yet read the original work or would like to read it again, get the book here.

Want to register yourself or a book group? It's free and takes 1-click.

Register here.

On the Next Page...

Please write us your reviews! Any length would be fine but we'd appreciate hearing you more! We'd be SO grateful.

Till next time,

BookHabits

"Loving Books is Actually a Habit"

CPSIA information can be obtained
at www.ICGtesting.com
Printed in the USA
LVHW090027090620
657704LV00001B/115